Start Orienteer

A scheme of work for primary teacl

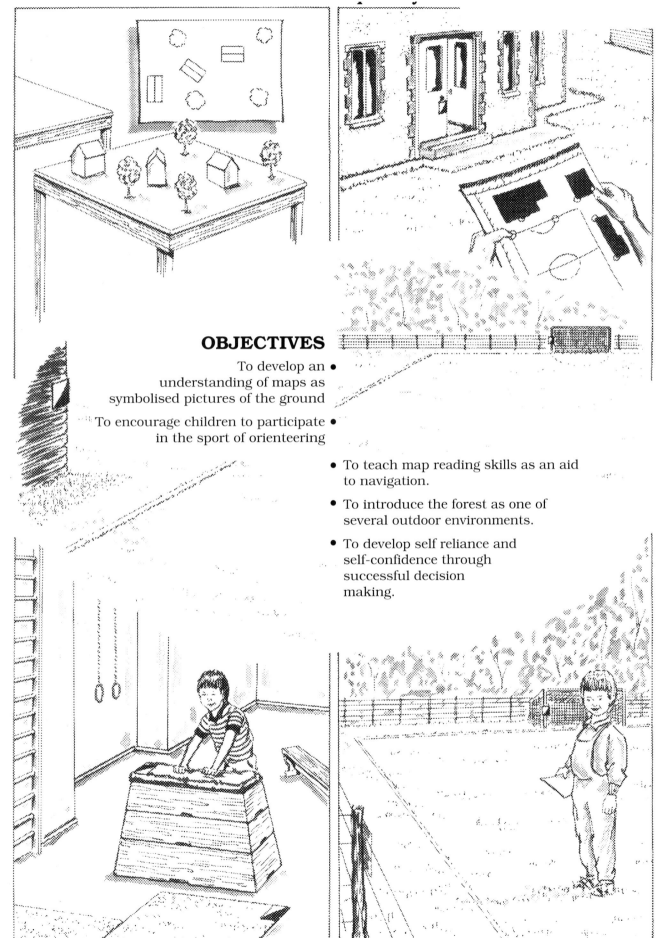

OBJECTIVES

- To develop an understanding of maps as symbolised pictures of the ground

- To encourage children to participate in the sport of orienteering

- To teach map reading skills as an aid to navigation.

- To introduce the forest as one of several outdoor environments.

- To develop self reliance and self-confidence through successful decision making.

LOOKING AT MAPS
CLASSROOM AND PLAYGROUND

OBJECTIVES
* *To enable children to acquire and extend the understanding of maps through practical activities.*

EQUIPMENT
Local map which includes the school, plus photocopies
8-10 mini/micro orienteering controls
A comprehensive selection of maps including -
city street plans, world map, atlas, physical maps, globe
Adhesive (blu-tak), string

KEY WORDS: PLANS • MAPS • SYMBOLS • ROUTE • ORIENTEERING • CONTROL

Teacher preparation
Hang up a display of maps. Place 8-10 controls in the playground, each with a code letter on it.

General introduction
Prior to the start of this block of work children should be encouraged to bring in a wide variety of maps and a colourful wall display should be made. Try to use a collection of orienteering maps for one corner of the display - contact your local orienteering club for help.

Discuss the different map sizes, colours and why and how maps are used. Introduce the idea of the map being an aerial or bird's-eye view of the ground. Each object or feature on the ground has a relationship with every other feature. This is reflected by the map. The map should be thought of as a picture with all the features seen in the same relationship or pattern as those on the ground. The map can be pictured as a 3-dimensional model or miniature of the landscape.

Discuss the use of symbols on maps. Use a road map to set tasks, e.g. the shortest routes between towns. Introduce the orienteering map. Explain the accuracy, detail and why it has been drawn, i.e. for a sport that involves running and map reading called orienteering. Show an orienteering control and a mini or micro-control.

Practical
Playground game: the teacher puts out 8-10 controls, using adhesive or string, on prominent features, e.g. gate, football post, steps, etc. They should be between knee and head height. No map is used.

The children find as many controls as they can in a given time, e.g. 5 minutes. They make a list of the letters on each control.

If you have a map of the school, help the children to identify where the controls were found.

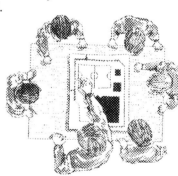

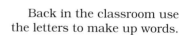

Back in the classroom use the letters to make up words.

OBJECTIVES
* *To build children's awareness and appreciation of maps through using them.*

EQUIPMENT
Local street or area map with school on it - one copy per child
Playground maps pre-marked with lesson 1 control sites
8-10 mini controls with code letters
Coloured cotton, chalk or crayons

KEY WORDS: ROUTE CHOICE • ORIENTEERING COURSE

Teacher preparation
Obtain maps. Place controls (with code letters) in the playground.

Classroom activity
Distribute local street or area maps. Ask the children to find the school, their own street, the nearest train/ bus station, a church, a supermarket etc. Have children draw in features not already included. Make a key if necessary and colour in the map if it is suitable.

Tasks - children locate their houses and work out the routes they take to school and other journeys.

Emphasise route choice. Children work out two or more routes between two places. Routes can be shown in different colours using chalk, crayons, cotton etc. The routes could be discussed using an OHP.

Explain that in the sport of orienteering runners often have a choice of route from one control to the next on the course.

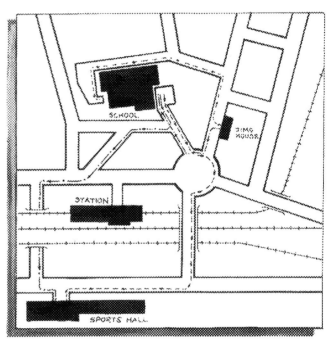

Hightlight the different routes

Practical
Distribute the playground maps with the controls marked on from lesson 1.

In the classroom, the children decide, as individuals or as pairs, which order they will find <u>all</u> the controls. They then go out and find them, copying each code letter on to their map.

The children then repeat this exercise but plan and visit the controls in a completely different order.

This exercise emphasises that the problem presented can be solved in different ways. On the second attempt running can be encouraged.

NB The next lesson focuses on setting the map. Reference could be made to 'setting' in this lesson if it is felt appropriate.

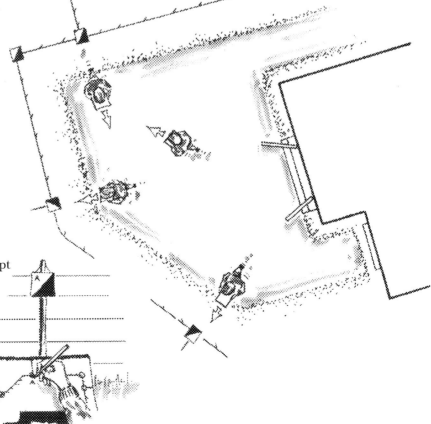

SYMBOLS AND SETTING THE MAP
CLASSROOM

OBJECTIVES
- *To introduce children to drawing their own simple maps*
- *To present the concept of keeping the map 'set' to read it*

EQUIPMENT
Pencils
Paper
Variety of objects for the desks

KEY WORDS: SETTING THE MAP • BIRDS EYE VIEW • MODEL

Teacher preparation
Collect the equipment.

Classroom activity
The teacher introduces or reminds the children of the concept of the map being a bird's eye view of the ground.

The children draw the outline of the teacher's desk and plot the objects on it, e.g. ruler, jar, rubber. ONLY use three or four objects at first and only add more when the drawings are accurate. Look at the relationship between one object and the others.

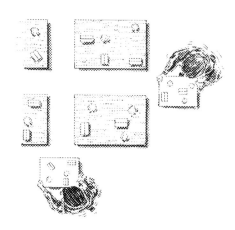

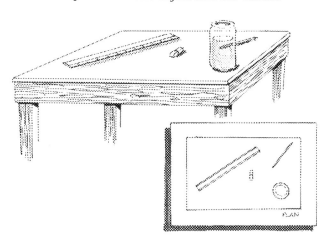

Show them how to SET the map so that as they face the desk the map lines up with the desk, the pattern of objects matching.

Fresh maps can be drawn using different objects.

Ask the children to approach their desks from different corners of the room. Ensure that the map is kept set as they change direction (ie. move the body round the map).

The children then draw an outline of their own desks or tables. They lay out objects and draw a plan of them.

THE MAP AS A PICTURE
CLASSROOM AND PLAYGROUND

OBJECTIVES
• *To develop an ability to draw a map.*
• *To promote understanding and to enhance the awareness of spatial relationships and symbols.*

EQUIPMENT
Mini-orienteering controls
Boards (to lean on)
Pencil, crayons
Paper
Doll

KEY WORDS: SCALE • NORTH • PICTURES • SYMBOLS

Teacher preparation
Draw an outline plan of the classroom on the blackboard. Put out controls.

Classroom activity
The children draw a map of the classroom showing desks, doors, windows, sink, blackboard, etc. See page 16 (maps). Omit individual chairs. Draw the room as a fly on the ceiling would see it. Cover the blackboard map so that the children do not copy it.

Discuss the use of symbols.

Suggest that the children colour in the map and then mark the North edge of the map with a red crayon. (This need not be precisely North). These map could be used for lesson 5.

Girl   Doll
scale 1:4

Scale
Discuss the scale of maps.

A map is drawn much smaller than full size.

Using a doll, measure its scale by counting how many dolls make up a child's height. If the ratio is 4 dolls to 1 child, the scale is 1:4.

Alternatively use metre sticks to measure the scale of the classroom map.

It is likely to be around 1:50
(2 cm per metre = 2cm:100cm = 2:100 = 1:50)

Reducing and enlarging the map on a photocopier can also be used to illustrate small and large scales.

Practical
In the playground the teacher puts out 6-10 controls with numbers. They must be on distinctive features i.e. gate post, end of flower bed, tree, steps, etc.

Give each child a number from one to ten then send them off with paper and board to find the control with their number.

They draw a picture of the control site, number it and return to the teacher. They repeat this with each control, collecting a clean piece of paper each time.

The pictures can be displayed in the classroom next to a playground map with the control circles on it.

⑤ SCORE ORIENTEERING
CLASSROOM AND GYM/HALL

OBJECTIVES
* *To introduce score orienteering using a classroom map*

EQUIPMENT
2 sets of matching cards (with different symbols drawn on)
Classroom maps
Blu-tak
Micro-markers
Paper and pencils

KEY WORDS: CROSS COUNTRY • SCORE ORIENTEERING

Teacher preparation
Photocopy a map of the classroom. Make one set of 10 cards with a different shape or map symbol on each card and **number** them. Make another identical set of 10 cards and put **letters** on them.

Classroom activity
Introduce the map of the classroom made by the teacher. Give one copy to each child.

Each pupil marks their place with a triangle. In orienteering the start is always shown by a triangle.

Mark the North edge of the map with a red crayon.

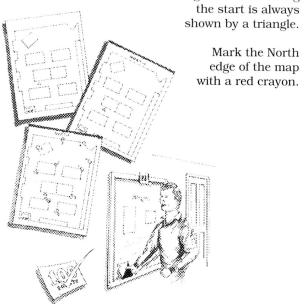

Place 10 lettered micro-markers, each on a different distinctive feature.

As each one is placed, the children mark the position on their maps with a clear circle in red and the number beside the circle, not in the middle of it. Do not allow the children to colour in the circles or the triangle otherwise the map detail will be hidden.

Teach map setting again. Make sure everything matches and Map North is always to the North end of the classroom.

Ask the children to find all the controls, in any order, and mark the letter found on each control beside the appropriate circle on their maps. They return to their seats when finished.

Give 10 points for each control (everyone should get 100 points).

During the exercise check that the children:
(i) do not just spot the controls by looking around but read the map to decide where they are.
(ii) keep the map set (move your body round the map).

Explain SCORE ORIENTEERING and show how it differs from CROSS COUNTRY ORIENTEERING.

Practical in the gymnasium/hall
Lay out the matching sets of cards on benches, one set at each end of the gymnasium. The children write numbers 1-10 on a piece of paper and then stand in the centre of the hall. Half of them face one bench, half the other.

The game is to run between the two benches matching the symbols and putting letters to numbers on the blank paper carried.

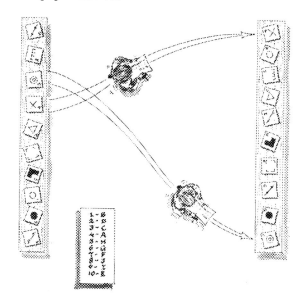

Announce the rules: No touching cards. One number/letter at a time. The winner is the one getting all the cards correct in the fastest time.

Increase the distance between the benches or play the game outside to increase the distance to run. Aim for about 10 minutes continuous running. More than one set of cards may be needed.

(A more complex version of this game is used with maps in lesson 6)

CROSS COUNTRY ORIENTEERING
CLASSROOM AND GYMNASIUM

OBJECTIVES
* *To improve basic fitness.*
* *To reinforce the concept of using a set or orientated map.*

EQUIPMENT
Orienteering maps with examples of cross country and score courses
Two sets of matching map cards
Classroom maps
Micro-markers with code letters

KEY WORDS: MASTER MAP • CROSS COUNTRY ORIENTEERING

Teacher preparation

Collect equipment. Make sets of cards. Mark up master maps - classroom maps with controls marked up neatly with a circle template.

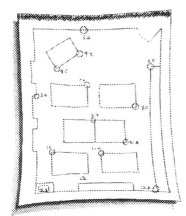

Classroom activity

Using the classroom map put out 10-12 coded micro markers on distinctive features of the room.

The children plot the markers (as in lesson 5) on their maps.

These controls could be used for another SCORE event - check maps are set as the children move around the classroom. Children mark codes on their own map as they reach them.

Then ask the children to join up 5-6 of the controls to make a CROSS COUNTRY COURSE on their own maps. Each uses his/her seat as the starting point (triangle) and numbers the controls in the order they are linked.

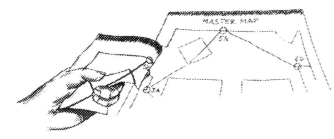

Working with a partner, the children change maps and walk each other's course checking that the codes are correct and visiting the controls in the correct sequence. Again check that the maps are kept set at every change of direction ("move your body round the map").

If there is extra time they can make up another cross country course using fresh maps.

Show orienteering maps with examples of a cross country and a score course.

Reinforce the use of symbols.

Practical in the gym

Make two sets of cards using pieces of the classroom or school map, similar to the cards used in lesson 5.

Cut two maps together making a simple jigsaw of 8-10 pieces. Stick the pieces on to card. Number the first set; put letters (at random) on the other. It helps to use different coloured card for each set.

Running game: matching the map pieces, as in lesson 5. Aim for 5/6 minutes' activity.

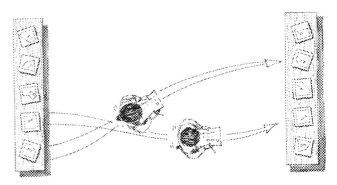

Master map copying

Each child has a map of the classroom or school without controls. Master maps are situated at one end of the hall and the children leave their own maps at the opposite end. They then run backwards and forwards remembering and copying one control at a time on to their own maps. Aim for 5/6 minutes' running.

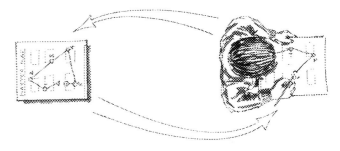

If this is too hard for some children, copying next to the master map is good practice.

Master maps

At most orienteering events each competitor has to copy his course from a master map on to his own map. This takes place immediately after the Start. Beginners can often copy their course before the Start.

7 MAKING A MAP
GYM OR HALL

OBJECTIVES
• *To draw and then use a map of the gym or hall*

EQUIPMENT
Gymnastic apparatus, e.g. mats, benches, hoops, box, etc
Paper
Rulers
Pencils
Red markers

KEY WORDS: MAPPING • SCALE • 'FOREST' • PLOTTING

Teacher preparation
Plan the layout of apparatus. Draw a
sample map.

Practical
*(in the Gym or defined
playground area such
as a netball court)*

Each child has an A4 sheet of
white paper, pencil and ruler.
Children with learning difficulties
should be given a copy of the plan
almost complete.

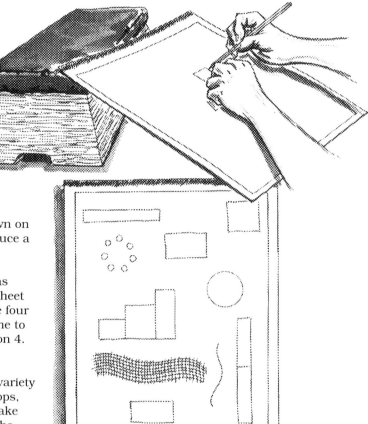

Ask the children to imagine they are looking down on
the area from the ceiling. They are going to produce a
map of the area.

Suggest the outline is drawn first. When this has
been completed, check to see that all of the A4 sheet
has been used. If some children have drawn the four
walls too small, use these different sizes of outline to
reinforce the concept of scale introduced in lesson 4.
Mark the North edge with red.

Create a 'forest' in the gym/hall by laying out a variety
of gymnastic equipment, e.g. mats, benches, hoops,
table, a badminton net (described as a river). Make
sure the initial 'forest' is quite simple and keep the
benches, boxes, mats parallel to the walls.

Teach the children to plot the features on to their
maps starting with the most obvious large feature in
the centre, then using this as the basis for fixing the
next feature.

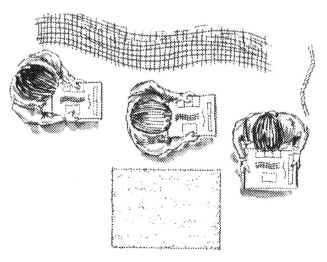

Using the apparatus laid out to make the
'forest', take the children for a 'forest' walk.
Suggest they keep the map set as they walk
through the 'forest'. The teacher should
demonstrate setting the map each time
direction is changed ("move your body
round the map").

The children can then work in pairs, taking
it in turn to lead.

Some children find it easier to put the 'set'
map down on the ground and move round
it, then pick it up ready to move on in the
new direction.

CROSS COUNTRY ORIENTEERING
GYM OR HALL

OBJECTIVES
• To encourage children to run a cross country course keeping the map set.
• To introduce children to a routine of thinking how to solve the navigational problems of getting from one point to the next.

EQUIPMENT
2 maps of gym/hall per child
Micro-markers
Red crayons

KEY WORDS: START • FINISH • CONTROL DESCRIPTIONS • USE THE MAP • WHERE AM I? • WHERE DO I WANT TO GO? • HOW DO I GET THERE?

Teacher preparation
Set out apparatus. Plan control sites for two courses.

Practical
Lay out the apparatus in the same pattern as lesson 7 to correspond with the children's maps.

The children scatter around the gym and find a space to sit.

They should mark their places on the map with a triangle in red.

The teacher puts out 6-8 micro markers each on a distinctive feature.

In orienteering each control has a written 'control description', helping the orienteer to find the controls. Give each of the gym controls a description as the markers are put out, Suggest or ask the children how each control site should be described.

e.g. N. end of box, junction of benches, centre of hoop, etc.

The children draw the circles then join them **all** up, in any order they choose, to make a cross-country course. The circles should be numbered in the order they will be visited. N.B. Each child will link them in a different order.

The children walk their own courses and write down the letter shown on the mini control beside the correct circle on the map. Use a red pen or crayon if possible.

Rules
• Use the map to locate the controls.
• Do not try to spot them by looking about the gym first.
• Keep the map set all the time.
• Move your body round the map.

Discuss the technique used to move from one control to the next.

Try to get the children to follow a thinking routine i.e. Where am I? Where do I want to go? How do I get there?

The first time they should walk round thinking through this routine.

Repeat this exercise with the children concentrating on reading the map as they run.

Link the children in pairs. They change maps and run their partner's course.

Collect the controls and then using fresh maps the children mark out a new course as the mini-markers are reset on different features. Use fewer markers this time but spread them out.

If there is time, suggest the children find a different starting point and repeat the exercises done so far in this lesson.

⑨ LINE ORIENTEERING
GYMNASIUM OR HALL

OBJECTIVES
- *To draw and use a new map of the hall.*
- *To practise map reading whilst running.*

EQUIPMENT
Apparatus in the gym
Pencils
Outline plans of the gym
Paper
Coloured pencils

KEY WORDS: LINE COURSE • CONCENTRATION

Teacher preparation
Plan the apparatus layout.

Practical
Lay out the apparatus similarly to lesson 8. This time use a greater variety of shapes. The long pieces, i.e. benches, need not be parallel to the walls. However, always start with a bench end or mat in the centre. An 'L' shape of two benches makes a good starting point.

Explain that a new 'forest' is going to be drawn. Each child has an outline plan of the gym, a pencil and ruler.

Plot each feature (as in lesson 7) starting from the centre.

Have some neat copies ready for the children having the greatest difficulty in drawing.

The teacher explains and demonstrates marking and following a **line course,** always keeping the map set.

Everyone is going to go on their own 'forest' walk, following a line (a route) which goes over, through and across the apparatus.

A line (in different coloured crayon) is to be drawn on the map showing the route taken during the 'forest' walk.

First sit everyone down to read their maps **concentrating** on the route they have just drawn and walked, imagining it in order to help remember it.

The children should walk their chosen routes stopping at each feature to draw in the line as they go, rather than run all the route then try to remember the course at the end.

Once the line has been marked on the map they can walk it or run it again, always keeping the map set.

The children are then going to watch their own routes being run or walked by someone else

Find a partner and change maps. One child then sits and watches the other following the line on the map. The observer is watching his own line being run. It is important that the runner uses the MAP to follow the line.

The two consult at the end discussing mistakes.

Then they change over. The observer becomes the runner.

Maps for lessons 11 and 12.
If there is not already a map of the school grounds, a map should be organised for use in the final lessons in this block. Use architect's plans of the school or a large scale (1:1250) Ordnance Survey map as the base. Help may be available from the Secondary School Geography or P.E. Departments or from the local Orienteering Club.

Remember that to copy any map, permission must be obtained from the copyright holder.

See MAPS p.16 for more information.

TREASURE HUNT
IN THE PLAYGROUND

OBJECTIVES
- *To construct and use small maps of parts of the playground or field.*
- *To compete in a score event.*

EQUIPMENT
'Treasure' e.g. class first names on pieces of card, or different coloured card, or pictures
'Big treasure' e.g. packet of Smarties
Paper
Pencils and crayons

KEY WORDS: TREASURE HUNT

Teacher preparation
Make 'treasure' name cards, and place them in the playground. Make a sample map of the area to be used. Make word cards describing the location of 'big treasure' (eg west, end, of, the, sports, field)

Practical 1
Take the children outside to a suitable part of the playground or school fields.

The children make a very simple map of this area containing very little other than a couple of buildings.

The emphasis, as in earlier mapping lessons, is on placing features in the right relationship to each other.

When the map is completed, play 'treasure hunt'.

The teacher has placed a number of pieces of 'treasure' on distinct places within the area of the map.

The children locate one piece of treasure at a time. The teacher marks an X on each child's map. The child uses it to find the right treasure. They leave the treasure in place and report back what they have found.

The children change maps and find new treasure using a map with a different x location on it.

Collect in these treasures.

Practical 2
The teacher then puts out the 'big treasure' location cards in the same area.

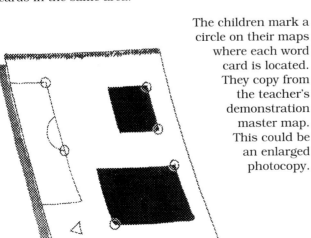

The children mark a circle on their maps where each word card is located. They copy from the teacher's demonstration master map. This could be an enlarged photocopy.

The children visit the control sites in any order, write down all the words then work out the message which indicates the location of the treasure, e.g. packet of Smarties.

They could work in pairs for this game

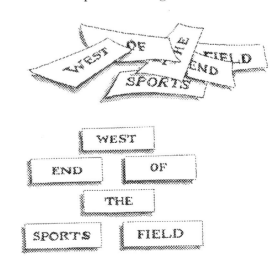

11 STAR EXERCISE
IN THE PLAYGROUND

OBJECTIVES
- *To introduce the new playground map.*
- *To reinforce setting the map.*
- *To help children maintain contact with the map as they move about.*

EQUIPMENT
Mini-markers with numbers and code letters
Red crayons/pens
Playground 'star' maps (2 for each control)
Pencils
Master code checklist

KEY WORDS: MAP CONTACT • SETTING THE MAP • STAR EXERCISE

Teacher preparation

Hang 8-10 mini-markers on definite features in the playground. Make two 'star' maps of each control with the start/base and one control only on each map.

These could be laminated for future use.

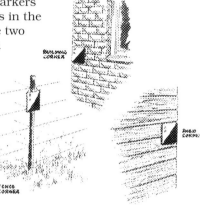

Practical

Using the playground map take the class for a map walk. Each child must have their own map.

Insist the map is correctly set and that the children are able to point to their position on the map whenever they stop.

NB Orienteers fold their maps and hold them with their thumbs beside their last known position. This is part of keeping **map contact**.

During the walk point out features and ask the children questions about map/terrain details. Ensure this is done slowly so that all children are always aware of their position on the map.

The walk should lead past the mini-markers which have been hung on definite features which are also on the map, e.g. fence **corner,** not just 'fence'.

Star exercise

This is one of the best orienteering exercises for teaching skills to mixed ability groups. Individuals can work at their own pace and the teacher is in contact with the whole class.

Each child will return to the base (triangle) after finding each control.

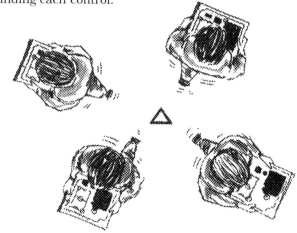

Number the children to indicate which control each one is to find first, e.g. number 6 goes to control 6 first.

Emphasise to the children that they must return after each control, remembering the code letter. The teacher checks that they have memorised the correct letter.

Each time the child returns to base they hand in the used map and take the next numbered map. The map must be set with the child facing the right direction ("move your body round the map") before they go to the new control. The teacher can give help to those who need it.

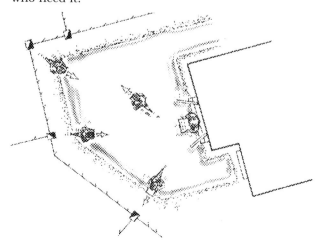

SCORE ORIENTEERING COMPETITION
IN THE PLAYGROUND

OBJECTIVES
• *To complete the block of work with a class competition.*

EQUIPMENT
10-15 mini-markers with numbers and letters
Master maps
Clock
Start banner
Watches useful

KEY WORDS: MASTER MAP • SCORE EVENT • THINKING SEQUENCE

Teacher preparation

Set up a score event hanging 10-15 mini-markers on distinctive features which are on the map. Each marker should be visible (not hidden) so that the children can find them by reading the map. Draw up 4-5 master maps.

Classroom

The children prepare for the score event by:

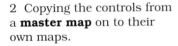

1 Drawing boxes in spaces round the outside edge of the front of the map, (not the back) so that the control code can be copied when each control is found.

2 Copying the controls from a **master map** on to their own maps.

Teach them to keep a finger pointing to the control on the master map when copying that control.

Practical

Set a time limit for the children to complete the course, eg 10-15 minutes. Explain that the purpose of the competition is to visit as many controls as possible within the time.

The controls can be visited in any order. Each control is worth a number of points (10 is the simplest) so they are trying to achieve as high a score as possible within the time. If they take longer then they will have points deducted for each minute late. A very lenient penalty would be minus 5 per minute as it would probably take less than a minute to return from the farthest point of the playground.

Remind the children of the skills needed to find controls successfully.

1 Keeping the map set.

2 Always knowing where they are on the map.

3 Remembering the thinking sequence 'Where am I? Where do I want to go? How do I get there?'

4 Deciding in which order they want to find the controls (in this score event).

Hold a mass start (everyone starts together). The children should complete the score event within the time limit. All the children should have been able to find all the controls.

Ring a bell or blow a whistle (3 rings/blasts) when there are one or two minutes to go. When time is up, one long ring/blast.

With nearly all the children gaining maximum scores the competitive element can be played down. Discussion can take place on route choice. Promote an atmosphere of enjoyment in completing the course to the best of one's ability (not to beat someone else for its own sake).

Children who ask if they can do more orienteering could be given an information sheet including the name and address of the local club secretary and the dates of the next local events.

EVALUATION

OBJECTIVES
• To evaluate the child's understanding of symbols and map orientation with changes of direction.

EQUIPMENT
Copies of plan A and B with questions
Model of plan

1 FEATURE RELATIONSHIPS

Map reading is about understanding the relationship of one feature with the others around it. This test, which can be written or oral, evaluates one aspect of this understanding.

Teacher preparation
Draw plans for the test. For younger children a model could be made to match the plan.

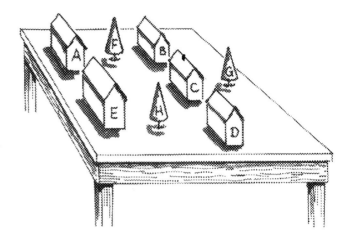

A With North at the top of the plan. Add the correct letter to complete each statement.

e.g. (1) H is next to E

   (2) ...... is between B and D

   (3) ...... is behind C

   (4) ...... is in front of B

   (5) ...... is between A and B

   (6) ...... is next to A

PLAN A

B With West at the top of the plan.

e.g. (1) B is behind C

   (2) ...... is next to G

   (3) ...... is between A and B

   (4) ...... is in front of A

   (5) ...... is behind C and D

   (6) ...... is between E and D

PLAN B

EQUIPMENT
6, or 12, cones
6, or 12, letters, one for each cone
North card
Route sheets and pencils

2 MAP ORIENTATION WITH CHANGES OF DIRECTION

Teacher preparation

Duplicate the route sheets, one per child. Using a hall or space outside, place 6 cones in two rows. Space them out at least one metre apart. Put a letter on each point and position the North card to indicate which side is north.

A duplicate cone 'grid' can be set up with a large group (more than 10).

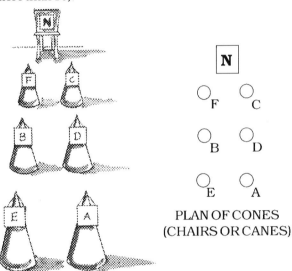

PLAN OF CONES
(CHAIRS OR CANES)

The test

- Each child has a route sheet with 10 routes and a pencil to copy down the letters.

- Demonstrate clearly how to complete each route:
  - SET the paper,
  - Locate the start cone,
  - Follow the first line to the next cone, write down the letter,
  - Continue following the route writing down the letters as you go,
  - When you have finished one route go on to the next.
  - Complete 5-8 different routes

- Number the group 1-10 so that they are starting on different routes. Use a second grid to ease congestion and allow more children to work at the same time.

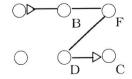

EXAMPLE OF ONE
COMPLETED
ROUTE

Having taught all the lessons in this book most of the class will achieve at least 50% correct routes Those with 50% or less should be given further help using the cones and then encouraged to do the routes again. This test can be used as part of a lesson for learning as well as evaluation.

THE ROUTE SHEET

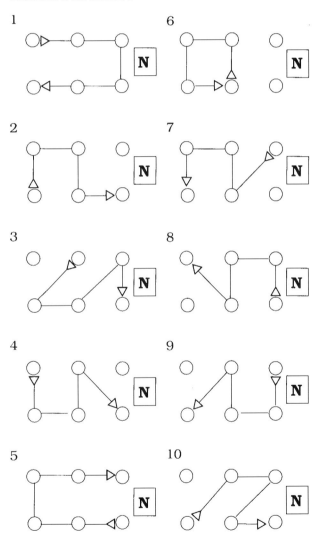

This test is adapted from one used by B.S. Wilson for a paper 'Navigational Skills and Strategies of Middle School Children' (University of Leeds). It originated as part of a test devised by by Semmes, Weinstein, Ghent and Teuber to investigate the effects of cerebral injury.

MAPS

CLASSROOM MAP

A large scale plan should include all the major fittings and fixtures. Leave out the chairs as these tend to clutter the map.

GYMNASIUM OR HALL MAP

With an outline PLAN drawn to scale (e.g. 1 pace = 2 cm) simple layouts of apparatus can be drawn by the pupils. Start from the CENTRE.

SCHOOL MAPS

A simple black and white school map can be easily made using a large scale Ordnance Survey map or Architects' plan as a base. Distinguish between walls,

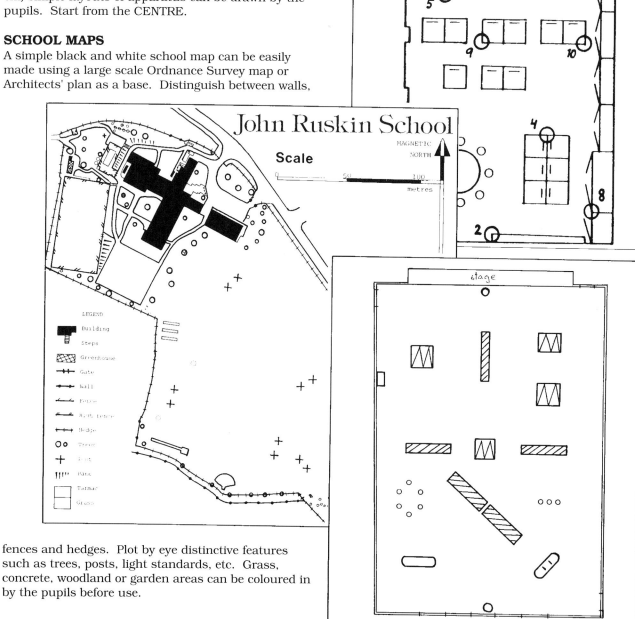

fences and hedges. Plot by eye distinctive features such as trees, posts, light standards, etc. Grass, concrete, woodland or garden areas can be coloured in by the pupils before use.

COLOURED MAPS

A coloured map of the school and grounds can often be obtained through collaboration with the nearest orienteering club. Many clubs have finance to promote orienteering in schools, and school/club links.

Alternatively, contact HARVEY who offer a professional mapmaking service.

COPYRIGHT

Remember that to copy any map, permission must be obtained from the copyright holder. BOF has an agreement with the OS for using their maps as a base. The map must bear a credit with specific wording and a licence number. Consult BOF Office for details.